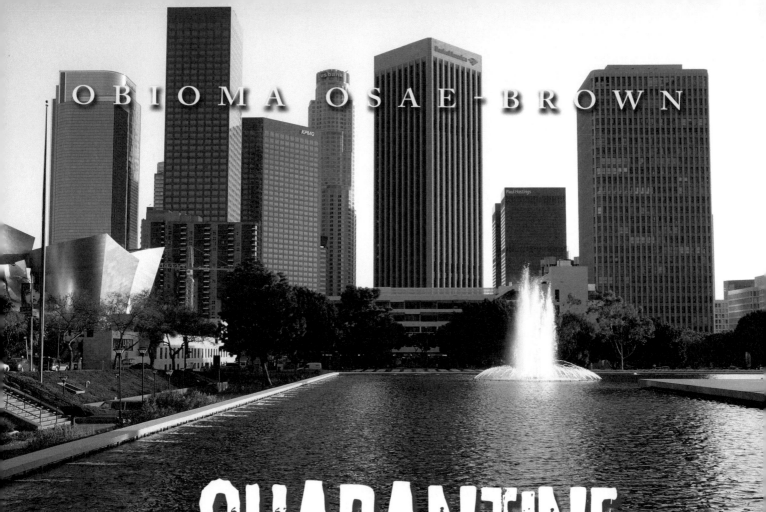

OBIOMA OSAE-BROWN

QUARANTINE
Reflections

AuthorHouse™
1663 Liberty Drive
Bloomington, IN 47403
www.authorhouse.com
Phone: 833-262-8899

Because of the dynamic nature of the Internet, any web addresses or links contained in this book may have changed
since publication and may no longer be valid. The views expressed in this work are solely those of the author and do
not necessarily reflect the views of the publisher, and the publisher hereby disclaims any responsibility for them.

This book is printed on acid-free paper.

Photo Credit for interior images: Jordan Osae-Brown

Cover Photo: Namibia Simba

ISBN: 978-1-6655-3008-8 (sc)
ISBN: 978-1-6655-3007-1 (e)

Library of Congress Control Number: 2021912805
Print information available on the last page.

Published by AuthorHouse 07/28/2021

authorHOUSE®

QUARANTINE
Reflections

Acknowledgement

I am surrounded daily by inspiration from faith, family, friends, and life events. I am grateful to my husband Isaac for his love, support, and critical input. I extend my gratitude to my son, Jordan, for his painstaking editorial ability, and the photos. For all those who liked or commented on my quotes each time they appeared on "My Story" or "What's on your mind?" on Facebook, I owe you a debt of gratitude. This book is dedicated to my daughter, Nanaba Osae-Brown: mom wants you to continue to be independent, sassy, and authentic. To all the girls and women who dare to challenge the status quo, I salute you!

About The Book

Ideas come from unexpected moments of inactivity. The pandemic created lots of free time to ponder and wonder, and often the mind was plagued with thoughts. The inspiration came from Facebook's caption page, "What's on your mind?." Initially, it started as simple quotes, a few "likes" and comments, but grew into "Quarantine Reflections."

The editing and photography for the book was done by my son, Jordan who had just finished a study abroad program at Osaka University, Japan, and graduated with a B.A. from University of California, Riverside.

It was a great way of inculcating the values of engagement, resilience, and vision. The pandemic has brought the toughest challenge in a generation, but has also brought the greatest stories of heroism, resiliency, camaraderie, and human dependency. As you ponder on the various thoughts in this book, it is hoped you will find, feel, and dwell on the things that influence us as humans, or the mantras to build character, integrity, and passion. The charge is to seize every opportunity in life as a call to make a difference.

Quotes about Life

No mortal has the ultimate power over any human, we are all subject to an end, usually sudden & terminal. The sooner we accept this truth, the sooner we can enjoy life to its fullest.

Perfection is not a human attribute. The desperate pursuit for continued perfection could be a recipe for disaster, brewing egotism, over confidence, & sloppiness.

When your life becomes overwhelming or begins to feel controlled, exercise self-love & empower yourself.

Knowledge is for everyone, but foolishness is for those who fight the unknown without trying to learn.

Humans are transient, temporal, & finite; everything passes with time.

Love runs deeper than can be fathomed and is always a recipe for peace and tranquility.

Human Frailty

Stockpiling hate, divisiveness, pain, & machiavellianism attest to the greed, insecurity, & depravity of humans.

Evil is corrosive, infectious, viral, & lethal, but it has an end.

The dark side of the power of choice, is the decision many make to follow people, systems, or institutions blindly.

Vengeance: toxic, unsettling, & lethal. Wise ones leave it to providence.

Attributes of mediocrity: pride, entitlement, ignorance, egocentrism, aggression, & control; a human deficit.

Control is often a disguise for weakness, fear, and insecurity.

You must love yourself truly, so that nothing upsets your essence or serenity. A broken glass only cuts.

Human Frailty II

Selfishness: denying others the opportunity, privileges, & positioning to emancipate themselves.

Why are we so quick to judge,
feel entitled, or validated;
or to assume the ultimate
relevance on earth?

What to do with fear? Ignore
it, confront it, & overcome it;
you have won already.

When we don't recognize our limitations, we forfeit our ability to be successful.

Constant micromanagement robs leaders of productive teams & streamlines the ability of teams to discover themselves.

Fear is an entrapment of the mind; those who succumb to it are oblivious to their true potential.

Knowledge

Education empowers us and breaks the barrier of ignorance.

The truth is never subjective; just give it time and be honest.

You have the freedom to choose.
Deceit, happiness, hate, love,
bitterness, joy, regret, or inertia.
It's your power!

Change is constant!

There is strength in diversity.

Knowledge

Ignorance is false confidence.

Being vulnerable is being human, so is being subjective and judgmental.

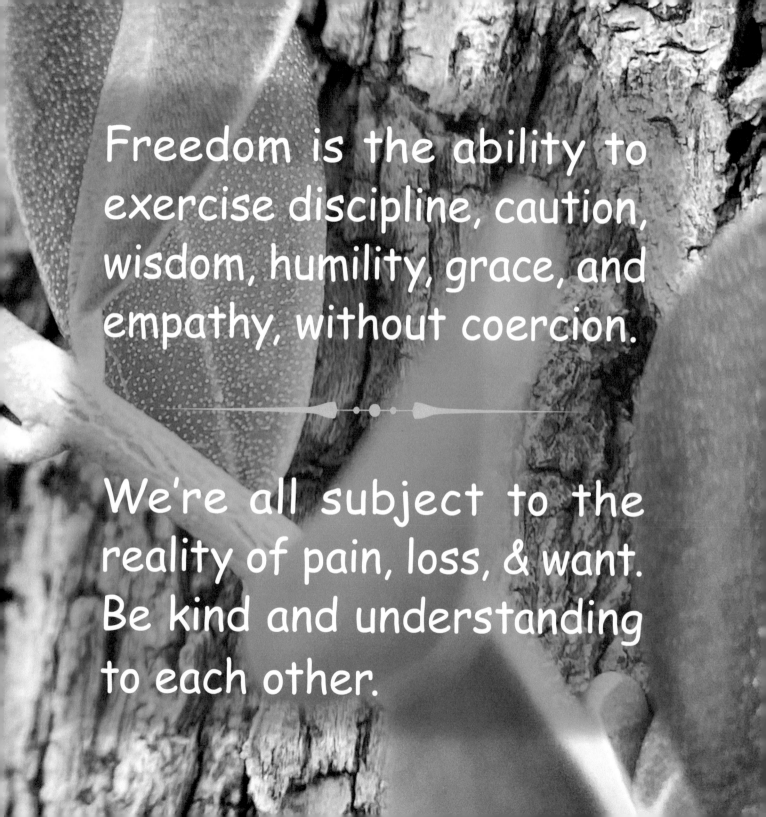

Freedom is the ability to exercise discipline, caution, wisdom, humility, grace, and empathy, without coercion.

We're all subject to the reality of pain, loss, & want. Be kind and understanding to each other.

Finance

Money that is not utilized to empower others, is like a lockdown: precautionary, laissez faire,& dormant.

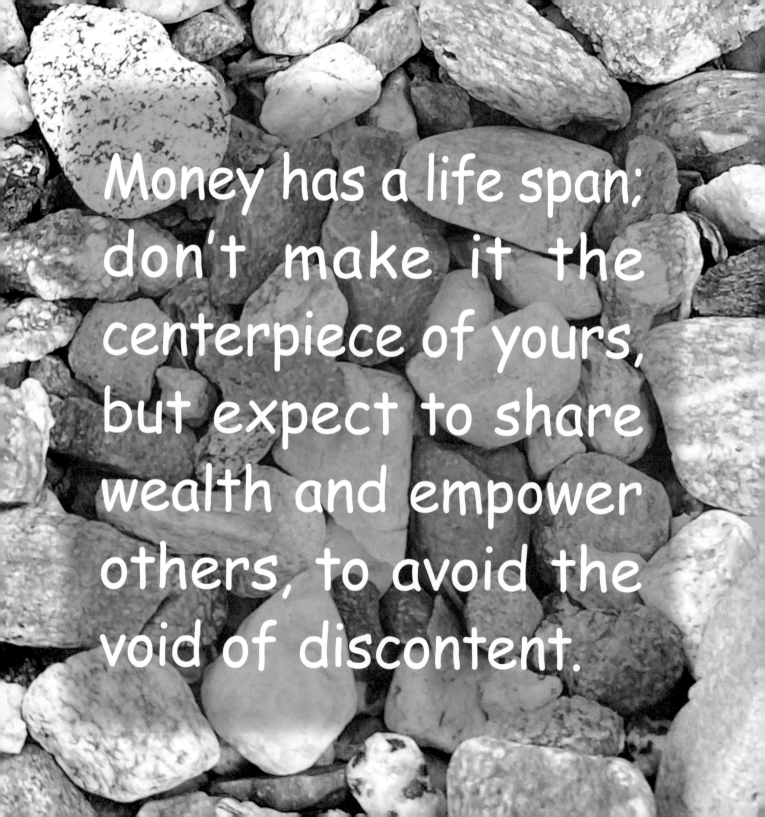

Money has a life span; don't make it the centerpiece of yours, but expect to share wealth and empower others, to avoid the void of discontent.

Compassion

Globalization is about humanity: one destiny and aspiration; let's support each other in the fight against egocentrism, selfishness, and injustice.

Service; the purest calling:
be selfless, unassertive,
empathetic, resilient, &
courageous.

Don't be so resolute in your
opinion until you have explored
all the facts. There is always
more than one side to a story.

Temperance: remember everything has its time & purpose. Won't you wear a mask even just to protect the most vulnerable?

Promote love as the epitome of freedom, devoid of egotism, coercion, & entitlement.

Does freedom give you the right to be selfish, conceited, or high-handed?

The intent to bring others down may be due to insecurities, esteem issues, or hate; free yourself from this and watch as life become more uplifting.

Ignorance and greed force people to look the other way while evil and hate run rampant.

The true judge of character is how you treat people when you are in charge.

It takes very little to be kind: a smile, a warm heart, humility, selflessness, empathy, & love.

To view critical humanitarian issues as "win" or "loss" situations; is debasing, ignorant, cruel, & a reflection of entitlement/privilege

Love runs deeper than can be fathomed: germane, authentic, surreal, and effective.

Faith

Absence of the right spiritual connection will keep us desolate & vulnerable.

Faith: celebrating success at the point of perceived failure.

⸻

Fear of the unknown breeds opportunity for the divine. Let your faith lead the way, and you will be protected.

Power of choice;
greatest gift to
man, but often
erroneously
exploited.

In the defining hour for humanity: let go, connect, & engage. Embrace goodwill, prayer, & love, instead of panic. Find a support system.

• • •

Religion and politics become hypocritical when they become selfish, manipulative, & draconian.

Divine intervention is closest when there's human degeneration; hold tight!

Everyone has a day of reckoning when all thoughts and deeds will be evaluated, assessed, and graded; be careful how the end plays out.

We should only be worried if the outcome of our lives is dependent on humans, fortunately it is not!

Root not for human justice, as it is often obscure, subjective, & fluid; instead, opt for divine justice: fair, thorough, & eternal.

Covid-19

A time to rest, reflect, heal, forgive, and reach out to each other. "physically" distancing; "emotionally" bonding.

Time out world: rest, reflect, reboot!

Right now is the perfect time to share, care, & love, the best antidote for boredom.

Heroes don't always have to be martyrs; provide our health professionals with essentials! #kits4healthworkers.

A successful quarantine will have left us embracing each other, becoming more accommodating to the differences in our lives, filled with love, selfless, and non-judgmental.

Printed in the United States
by Baker & Taylor Publisher Services